OUR APPOINTMENT with LIFE

OUR APPOINTMENT with LIFE
The Buddha's Teaching on Living in the Present

Translation and Commentary on
The Sutra on Knowing the Better Way to Live Alone

THICH NHAT HANH

Parallax Press
Berkeley, California

Parallax Press
P.O. Box 7355
Berkeley, California 94707

Translated from the Vietnamese by Annabel Laity
Cover drawing by Nguyen Thi Hop
Cover design by Gay Reineck
Composed on Macintosh by Parallax Press

ISBN 0-938077-36-8

Contents

*"Our appointment with life
is in the present moment.
The place of our appointment
is right here, in this very place."*

Part One

The Sutras

The Elder Sutra
Theranamo Sutta
Translated from the Chinese

I heard these words of the Buddha one time when the Lord was staying at the monastery in the Jeta Grove, in the town of Sravasti. At that time there was a monk named Thera (Elder), who always preferred to be alone. Whenever he could, he praised the practice of living alone. He sought alms alone and sat in meditation alone.

One time a group of bhikkhus came to the Lord, paid their respect by prostrating at his feet, stepped to one side, sat down at a distance, and said, "Blessed One, there is an elder by the name of Thera who only wants to be alone. He always praises the practice of living alone. He goes into the village alone to seek alms, returns home from the village alone, and sits in meditation alone."

The Lord Buddha told one of the bhikkhus, "Please go to the place where the monk Thera lives and tell him I wish to see him."

The bhikkhu obeyed. When the monk Thera heard the Buddha's wish, he came without delay, prostrated at the feet of the Buddha, stepped to one side, and sat down at a distance. Then the Blessed One asked the monk Thera, "Is it true that you prefer to be alone, praise the life of solitude, go for alms alone, come back from the village alone, and sit in meditation alone?"

The monk Thera replied, "It is true, Blessed One."

Buddha asked the monk Thera, "How do you live alone?"

The monk Thera replied, "I live alone; no one else lives with me. I praise the practice of being alone. I go for alms alone, and I come back from the village alone. I sit in meditation alone. That is all."

The Buddha taught the monk as follows, "It is obvious that you like the practice of living alone. I do not want to deny that, but I want to tell you that there is a wonderful way to be alone. It is the way of deep observation to see that the past no longer exists and the future has not yet come, and to dwell at ease in the present moment, free from desire. When a person lives in this way, he has no hesitation in his heart. He gives up all anxieties and regrets, lets go of all binding desires, and cuts the fetters which prevent him from being free. This is called 'the better way to live alone.' There is no more wonderful way of being alone than this."

Then the Blessed One recited this gatha:

> In observing life deeply,
> it is possible to see clearly all that is.
> Not enslaved by anything,
> it is possible to put aside all craving.
> The result is a life of peace and joy.
> This is truly to live alone.

Hearing the Lord's words, the monk Thera was delighted. He prostrated respectfully to the Buddha and departed.

From the Agamas (Samyukta 1071). The equivalent in the Pali Canon is the Theranamo Sutta (Samyutta Nikaya 21.20).

The Sutra on Knowing
the Better Way to Live Alone
Bhaddekaratta Sutta
Translated from the Pali

I heard these words of the Buddha one time when the Lord was staying at the monastery in the Jeta Grove, in the town of Sravasti. He called all the monks to him and instructed them, "Bhikkhus!"

And the bhikkhus replied, "We are here."

The Blessed One taught, "I will teach you what is meant by 'knowing the better way to live alone.' I will begin with an outline of the teaching, and then I will give a detailed explanation. Bhikkhus, please listen carefully."

"Blessed One, we are listening."

The Buddha taught:

> Do not pursue the past.
> Do not lose yourself in the future.
> The past no longer is.
> The future has not yet come.
> Looking deeply at life as it is
> in the very here and now,
> the practitioner dwells
> in stability and freedom.
> We must be diligent today.
> To wait until tomorrow is too late.
> Death comes unexpectedly.
> How can we bargain with it?
> The sage calls a person who knows
> how to dwell in mindfulness
> night and day
> "one who knows
> the better way to live alone."

"Bhikkhus, what do we mean by 'pursuing the past'? When someone thinks about the way his body was in the past, the way his feelings were in the past, the way his perceptions were in the past, the way his mental factors were in the past, the way his consciousness was in the past; when he thinks about these things and his mind is burdened by and attached to these things which belong to the past, then that person is pursuing the past.

"Bhikkhus, what is meant by 'not pursuing the past'? When someone thinks about the way his body was in the past, the way his feelings were in the past, the way his perceptions were in the past, the way his mental factors were in the past, the way his consciousness was in the past; when he thinks about these things but his mind is neither enslaved by nor attached to these things which belong to the past, then that person is not pursuing the past.

"Bhikkhus, what is meant by 'losing yourself in the future'? When someone thinks about the way his body will be in the future, the way his feelings will be in the future, the way his perceptions will be in the future, the way his mental factors will be in the future, the way his consciousness will be in the future; when he thinks about these things and his mind is burdened by and daydreaming about these things which belong to the future, then that person is losing himself in the future.

"Bhikkhus, what is meant by 'not losing yourself in the future'? When someone thinks about the way his body will be in the future, the way his feelings will be in the future, the way his perceptions will be in the future, the way his mental factors will be in the future, the way his consciousness will be in the future; when he thinks about these things but his mind is not burdened by or daydreaming about these things which belong to the future, then he is not losing himself in the future.

"Bhikkhus, what is meant by 'being swept away by the present'? When someone does not study or learn anything about the Awakened One, or the teachings of love and understanding, or the community that lives in harmony and awareness; when that person knows nothing about the noble teachers and their teachings, and does not practice these teachings, and thinks, 'This body is myself; I am this body. These feelings are myself; I am these feelings. This perception is myself; I am this perception. This mental factor is myself; I am this mental factor. This consciousness is myself; I am this consciousness,' then that person is being swept away by the present.

"Bhikkhus, what is meant by 'not being swept away by the present'? When someone studies and learns about the Awakened One, the teachings of love and understanding, and the community that lives in harmony and awareness; when that person knows about noble teachers and their teachings, practices these teachings, and does not think, 'This body is myself; I am this body. These feelings are myself; I am these feelings. This perception is myself; I am this perception. This mental factor is myself; I am this mental factor. This consciousness is myself; I am this consciousness,' then that person is not being swept away by the present.

"Bhikkhus, I have presented the outline and the detailed explanation of knowing the better way to live alone."

Thus the Buddha taught, and the bhikkhus were delighted to put his teachings into practice.

Bhaddekaratta Sutta (Majjhima Nikaya 131)

Part Two

The Subject Matter of the Sutras

During the time of the Buddha, there was a bhikkhu named Ekavihariya, who liked to live alone. Literally, his name means "One (*eka*) Living (*vihariya*)." It is possible that he received this ordination name because he was so calm and practiced mindfulness so well. The Buddha once praised him with this short gatha:

> Sitting alone, resting alone,
> going forth alone, without laziness;
> he who understands deeply
> the roots of suffering
> enjoys great peace,
> while dwelling in solitude.

This gatha is in the *Dhammapada*. The monk Ekavihariya was well-loved and respected by his fellow practitioners. Some gathas written by him can be found in the *Theragatha* (*Poems of the Elder Monks*), verses 537-546. In these poems, he praises the tranquillity of living alone.

There was another monk, named Thera (Elder), who also liked to live alone and often spoke highly of the solitary life. However this monk was not praised by his fellow practitioners or by the Buddha. Perhaps he had heard that the practice of being alone was commendable, and he wanted to practice living alone. But he lived the solitary life only according to the outer form, and his fellow practitioners noticed there was something unbalanced about it. They told the Buddha about him, and the Buddha invited Thera to come see him. When Thera presented himself, the Buddha asked him, "People say that you like living alone and that you praise the practice of solitude. Is that true?"

The monk replied, "Yes, Lord, it is true."

The Buddha asked, "What is your way of living alone?"

Thera replied, "I walk into the village for alms alone. I leave the village alone, and I come back to the monastery alone. I eat the midday meal alone. I practice sitting meditation alone."

The Buddha said, "Monk Thera, it is true that you live alone. I cannot deny that. But I want to tell you a way to live alone that is much more enjoyable, much more deep and wonderful."

Then the Buddha taught him, "Let go of what is past. Let go of what is not yet. Observe deeply what is happening in the present moment, but do not be attached to it. This is the most wonderful way to live alone."

This conversation, so similar to the one quoted on page 3 from the *Agamas* (*Samyukta 1071*), is from the *Theranamo Sutta* (*Samyutta Nikaya 21.20*).

I believe that after the monk Thera heard the Buddha's teaching, he changed his way of living alone. The Buddha taught that being in the present moment is the way to live alone. If a person cannot live mindfully in the present moment, then even if he or she is all alone in the forest, it is not truly living alone. But if someone lives mindfully in the present moment, not regretting the past and not anxious about the future, he or she knows how to observe and understand what is happening in the present. I believe that the Bhikkhu Thera learned this and put it into practice after it was taught to him by the Buddha.

The title of the first sutra, *Theranamo*, means "The One Named Thera." Thera was probably not the monk's ordination name. Thera simply means "elder." It is possible that after the Buddha taught Thera the contents of this sutra, the other monks, out of respect for him, began to refer to him in the sutra as the Elder, rather than by his prior name.

As the Buddha taught, a person who knows the better way to live alone does not necessarily live isolated from society. To put society at a distance and to live isolated in the forest is no guarantee of being alone. If we continue to go back to the past, worry about the future, or drown in the distractions of the present, we can never be alone. One who knows the better way to live alone can do so right in society.

This is also made quite clear in the *Migajala Sutta* (*Samyutta Nikaya 35, 63-64*). At that time the Buddha was residing in Campa, on the shore of the lake. A monk named Migajala came to see him. He had already heard about the teaching of the better way to live alone, and he came to ask the Buddha about it.

The Buddha instructed Migajala, "The forms and images which are the objects of our vision can be pleasant, enjoyable, and memorable, and can lead to craving and desire. If a monk is attached to them, then he is bound by them, and he is not alone. He is always with another."

The expression "being with another" is translated from the word *sadutiyavihari*. It is the opposite of "living alone." But when the Buddha used this word, he did not mean that the monk was living with other people. He meant that a monk who is bound by any objects, even objects of consciousness, is, in fact, living with those objects.

The Buddha added, "Indeed, Migajala, if a monk is bound by any fetter like this, even if he lives deep in the forest, in a deserted place without others, and without any outer disturbance, he still lives with another. Why? Because he has still not thrown off the fetters that bind him. Those fetters are the ones with whom he lives."

Buddha taught Migajala that a person who knows the better way to live alone is someone who lives at ease, not bound by the internal formations which are based in the objects of the six senses, i.e. in form, sound, smell, taste, touch, and the objects of the mind.

The Buddha concluded, "Migajala, if a monk lives like this, even in the center of a village; with monks, nuns, or lay practitioners; among royalty, or high-ranking officials; or with those who practice another way, he is still someone who knows the better way to live alone. He can be said to be living alone because he has freed himself from all attachments.

On another occasion, in Anathapindika's park, the Buddha called the monks together and taught them the gatha which summarized the important points on the better way to live alone. This is the subject matter of the *Bhaddekaratta Sutta* (*Sutra On Knowing the Better Way to Live Alone*). This poem became well-known and is found in many other sutras as well. In the *Madhyamagama* of the Chinese canon, there are three sutras which quote this gatha. The first is *The God of the Forest Hot Springs Sutra* (no. 165), in which the poem is quoted four times. The second is *The Shakyan Hermitage Sutra* (no. 166), in which the gatha is quoted three times. The third sutra is the *Sutra Spoken by Ananda* (no. 167), in which the gatha is quoted once.

In the Pali Canon, I have come across four suttas with the "Bhaddekaratta" gatha, all in the *Majjhima Nikaya*. The first is the *Bhaddekaratta Sutra* (M131). The second is the *Ananda-Bhaddekaratta* Sutra (M132), which is the equivalent of the *Sutra Spoken by Ananda*. The third is the *Mahakaccana-Bhaddekaratta Sutra* (M133), equivalent to *The God of the Forest Hot Springs Sutra*. The fourth is the *Lomasakangiya-Bhaddekaratta Sutra* (M134),[1] equivalent to the *Shakyan Hermitage Sutra*.

Knowing the better way to live alone is an important subject for Buddhism. It shines light on the essence of living in an awakened way as taught by the Buddha: to let go of the past and the future, and to live mindfully in order to look deeply and discover the true nature of all that is taking place in the present moment. Besides the four Pali suttas and three Chinese sutras mentioned above, the subject of living alone is referred to in many other places in the canons (although the "Bhaddekaratta"

---

[1] The *Lomasakangiya-Bhaddekaratta* has a second translation in the Chinese Canon. This is the *Sutra of Great Reverence* which is no. 77 in the *Taisho Revised Tripitaka*. The translator is Dharmapala (Truc Phap Ho) of Yueh Chih (Indo-Scythia).

gatha is not used). For example, it is the subject of the *Theranamo* and the *Migajala* sutras, which we have quoted above.

The terms *ekavihari* (one who lives alone) and *sadutiyavihari* (one who lives with another) in the *Migajala Sutta* are easy to understand and accept. But the term *bhaddekaratta* is difficult to translate. Dharmanandi, who translated the *Samyukta-gama* into Chinese, did not understand this compound word, so he just transcribed it into Chinese characters and used it as the title of the gatha.[2]

A number of Buddhist masters of the Southern Tradition understand *ekaratta* as "one night" and translate *Bhaddekaratta* as "A Good Night for Meditation." Judging from the content of the sutra, I believe this translation is not correct. *Bhadda* means "good" or "ideal." *Eka* means "one" or "alone." *Ratta* means "to like." The contemporary Buddhist scholar Bhikkhu Nanananda, translates the title as "The Ideal Lover of Solitude." After much reflection, I think that "Knowing the Better Way to Live Alone" is closer to the original meaning of the sutra.

The gatha, also entitled "Knowing the Better Way to Live Alone," was composed by the Buddha to summarize what he had just taught the monks

---

[2] Master Dharmapala translated *Bhaddekaratta* as *Xián Shàn. Xián* means "virtuous" or "able," *shàn* means "good," "good at," or "skillful." These two words translate *bhadda* and *ratta*. But the part *eka*, "alone," which lies between *bhadda* and *ratta*, has been overlooked, although it is fundamental to the meaning of the compound.

Thera and Migajala. The Buddha read this gatha to the monks in the Jetavana monastery and later commented on it for them. The opening paragraphs of the sutra depict the occasion on which the *Sutra On Knowing the Better Way to Live Alone* was delivered.

The people who were able to hear the Buddha that day were limited to the monks who were present in the Jetavana monastery. Because of the importance of the subject, monks and nuns living elsewhere gradually came to know about the "Knowing the Better Way to Live Alone" gatha. *The God of the Forest Hot Springs Sutra* tells us: "At that time the Buddha was staying in Rajagriha at the Venuvana monastery. The monk Samiddhi was residing in the nearby forest. One morning after bathing in the hot springs, Samiddhi was putting on his robe, when a beautiful god appeared, prostrated before him, and asked him if he had ever heard and practiced the "Knowing the Better Way to Live Alone" gatha. The god said, "Venerable Samiddhi, you should ask the Buddha to teach us this gatha so that we can put it into practice. I have heard that this gatha contains the deepest meaning of the Buddha's teachings, that it is the basis for the enlightened life, and that it can lead to awakened understanding and *nirvana*." After the god had spoken, he joined his palms and walked clockwise three times around the monk to show his respect.

The monk Samiddhi went to the Buddha. After prostrating to the Awakened One, he told about his encounter with the god and asked the Buddha to teach him the "Knowing the Better Way to Live Alone" gatha. Buddha asked Samiddhi if he knew who the god was. When Samiddhi replied that he did not, Buddha told him the god's name and that he came from the thirty-third heaven. Then Samiddhi and the monks who were present asked the Buddha again to teach them the gatha. Buddha recited it for them:

> Do not pursue the past.
> Do not lose yourself in the future.
> The past no longer is.
> The future has not yet come.
> Looking deeply at life as it is
> in the very here and now,
> the practitioner dwells
> in stability and freedom.
> We must be diligent today.
> To wait until tomorrow is too late.
> Death comes unexpectedly.
> How can we bargain with it?
> The sage calls a person who knows
> how to dwell in mindfulness
> night and day
> "one who knows
> the better way to live alone."

After reciting the gatha, the Buddha left his seat and returned to his hut to meditate. The monks, including Samiddhi, wished to hear an explanation of it, so they went to the elder Kaccana, a senior disciple of the Buddha, recited the gatha to him, and asked if he would comment on it. The monk Kaccana was known to have many excellent qualities. He was often praised by the Buddha for his intelligence, and the monks thought he would be able to offer a penetrating explanation. At first Kaccana hesitated. He suggested that the monks go directly to the Buddha, so that the commentary be from the Teacher himself. But, in the end, because the bhikkhus insisted, he agreed to explain the gatha to them. This elder's commentary is the essential content of *The God of the Forest Hot Springs Sutra.*

After offering this explanation of the gatha, the elder told the monks that if the opportunity presented itself, they should ask Buddha to explain it directly, because his own insight could never be as profound as the insight of the Awakened One.

The bhikkhus, including Samiddhi, did have another audience with the Buddha, and they told the Buddha the explanation of the "Knowing the Better Way to Live Alone" gatha that they had heard from Kaccana. The Buddha began by speaking in praise of the elder: "Excellent. Among my disciples there are those who grasp the meaning of the Dharma and understand its significance. If the teacher recites a gatha and does not have a chance to comment on it, then it is the disciples who must penetrate the meaning of the gatha and give a fuller explanation of the teaching. The Elder Kaccana is a senior bhikkhu. The commentary he gave you shows the true meaning of the gatha and is in accord with the truth of the way things are. You should use it and make it part of your practice."

This exchange took place in Rajagriha, the capital city of Magadha, on the left bank of the Ganges. The account which follows took place further north, in the town of Sravasti, the capital of the kingdom of Kosala, on the right bank of the

Ganges. That account is given in the *Shakyan Hermitage Sutra.*

The Shakyan Hermitage had been built by members of the Shakyan clan in the hills not far from Sravasti. This hermitage also had the name "No Problems" or "At Peace." At that time, the bhikkhu Lomasakangiya was staying in the hermitage. One night, shortly before daybreak, he stepped outside and spread out a cloth on one of the string cots under the trees. As soon as he began to sit on the cot in the lotus position, a very beautiful god appeared, prostrated before him, and asked if he knew the "Knowing the Better Way to Live Alone" gatha and if he had ever heard a commentary on it. The monk in turn asked the god the same question, and the god replied that he had heard the gatha but he had not yet had the chance to hear the commentary explaining the deep meaning of the gatha. The elder asked, "How is it that you have heard the gatha but have not yet heard the commentary?"

The god explained that at one time, when the Buddha was residing in Rajagriha, he had heard the Buddha recite the gatha, but the Buddha had given no commentary.

Then the god recited the gatha and advised the monk to go and ask the Buddha to explain it. The gatha in this sutra is identical with the one in the *The God of the Forest Hot Springs Sutra.*

After that, the bhikkhu Lomasakangiya went to the Buddha and told him what had happened. At that time, the Buddha was staying in the Jetavana monastery in Sravasti. Having heard the account, the Buddha told Lomasakangiya that the name of the god who had appeared to him was Candana

(Sandalwood) and that he came from the thirty-third heaven. Then bhikkhu Lomasakangiya requested the Buddha to explain the gatha.

That day, there were many bhikkhus present. The Buddha's commentary on the gatha forms the essence of the *Shakyan Hermitage Sutra* (*Madhyamagama* 166, which is the equivalent of the *Lomasakangiya-Bhaddekaratta,* no. 134 in the *Majjhima Nikaya*). As we have seen, there is a second Chinese version of this sutra translated by Dharmapala entitled *The Sutra of Great Reverence.* Comparing the two sutras is very interesting and can help us understand many details of the story.

The final sutra I will cite is the *Sutra Spoken by Ananda.* The Buddha delivered this discourse at Sravasti. One night the Venerable Ananda asked the monks to assemble in the main Dharma hall of the Jetavana monastery, and he recited and explained the "Knowing the Better Way to Live Alone" gatha. Early the next day, one of the bhikkhus went to see the Buddha and told him about Ananda's Dharma talk. The sutra does not say that the bhikkhu expressed any lack of confidence in the Venerable Ananda, but the sutra does say that after the Buddha heard about the Dharma talk, he sent the bhikkhu to invite Ananda to join them.

When Ananda arrived in the Buddha's room, the Buddha asked him, "Is it true that you recited and gave a talk on the gatha, 'Knowing the Better Way to Live Alone' last night?"

Ananda replied that it was true, and the Buddha asked, "Can you recite it for me and tell me your commentary on it?"

After Ananda recited the gatha and told the Buddha his explanation of it, the Buddha asked Ananda several more questions. When he heard Ananda's answers, he praised him, saying, "Excellent! Among my disciples there are those who have the insight to understand the essential significance of the teachings."

Buddha praised Ananda in the way that he had praised Kaccana. On that day there were many bhikkhus present, among them the bhikkhu who had told the Buddha about Ananda's Dharma talk. Perhaps the Buddha spoke those words to assure the monks that the Venerable Ananda's grasp of the Dharma was as firm as Kaccana's and that the bhikkhus could make Ananda's teachings a part of their practice. The main part of the *Sutra Spoken by Ananda*[3] is comprised of the answers given by Ananda to the Buddha's questions.

---

[3] *Madhyamagama* 167, equivalent to the *Ananda-Bhadde-karatta* in the Pali Canon.

Part Three

Putting the Teachings of the Buddha into Practice

Not to Reject the World and Society

To live alone does not mean to reject the world and society. The Buddha said that living alone means living in the present moment deeply observing what is happening. If we do that, we will not be dragged into the past or swept away into thoughts about the future. The Buddha said that if we cannot live in the present moment, even if we are alone in the deepest forest, we are not really alone. He said that if we are fully alive in the present moment, even if we are in a crowded, urban area, we can still be said to be living alone.

Buddhist meditators know the importance of practicing in a community. That is the meaning of the phrase, "I take refuge in the sangha." A Vietnamese proverb goes: "Soup is to a meal what friends are to the practice." To be in touch with a community, to learn from its members, and to take refuge in a community is very important. To discover the way of being alone in a practice community is something we need to do.

The monk Thera was part of a practice community, but he was determined to live alone. He believed in the idea of a solitary life, because he had at some time heard the Buddha praising the practice of living alone. So he kept his distance from everyone else. He begged for alms alone, he returned alone, he ate alone, and he meditated alone. He was like a drop of oil in a bowl of water, unable to mix with his fellow practitioners. Because of this, the other bhikkhus thought there was something abnormal about him, and they expressed their concern to the Buddha.

The Buddha was very kind. He did not criticize Thera. He only said that Thera's way of living alone was not the best way of doing so. Because many other monks were present, Buddha took the opportunity to teach Thera the better way of living alone—a way in which it is still possible to associate with the sangha of bhikkhus, to learn from and take refuge in them.

There were bhikkhus who were the opposite of Thera who would always gather in small groups and fritter away their time chatting and joking. Their conversations were not about the teachings, and the Buddha frequently reprimanded them. There are stories throughout the sutras in which the Buddha advises or chides the bhikkhus who act in a noisy and undisciplined way, not knowing how to keep body and mind in check, not knowing how to spend their time usefully in practicing walking and sitting meditation and observing deeply things as they are in the present moment. *The Nagita Sutta* (*Anguttara Nikaya* V 30, VI 42, VIII 86) is one of the discourses in which the Buddha speaks about this. (In the Chinese Canon, see nos. 1250 and 1251 of the *Samyuktagama*.)

When I first became a monk, my master gave me a copy of the book, *Words of Discipline of Master Quy Son*. I will never forget the sentences in which Master Quy Son reprimands practitioners who, after the midday meal, gather in small groups and talk about meaningless things. Quy Son's words of advice have often come back to me and served as a reminder.

When we live in a practice community, there should always be at least one or two people who serve as role models. Sometimes we only need to watch them standing, walking, speaking, or smiling in mindfulness, and we feel steady in our own practice. The fact that we know "the better way to live alone" does not prevent us from enjoying and benefitting from the presence of such people. On the contrary, it is because we know "the better way to live alone" that we have the ability to observe them deeply and appreciate them.

To be in touch does not mean just to talk with the other person. When we are in touch with the blue sky, for example, the white clouds, the green willow, or the rose, we do not communicate with them only in words. We recognize and accept these things, and feel their warmth. Confidence springs up in us, and we learn a lot from their presence. In this way we are able to profit from the third jewel, the practice community.

If we practice "the better way of living alone," and we spend most of our time quietly practicing walking and sitting meditation, our presence will make a real contribution to the community. Unlike the monk Thera or the monks who gather after meals to talk about things that are not important, every step we make adds to the quality and stability of the practice in the community. We are like Shariputra, Kashyapa, Badhya, or Kimbila—all students of the Buddha. Seeing us, the Buddha will be satisfied and smile. The Buddha knows that if every individual in the community knows how to live alone, the quality of life in the community will be excellent. When all the members of the community contribute to that quality, the community has a strong foundation, and many people can benefit from it. To live alone means to live in mindfulness. It does not mean to isolate oneself from society. If we know the better way to live alone, we can be in real touch with people and society, and we will know what to do and what not to do to be of help.

The Richness of the Spiritual Life Comes from Living Alone

If we live in forgetfulness, if we lose ourselves in the past or in the future, if we allow ourselves to be tossed about by our desires, anger, and ignorance, we will not be able to live each moment of our life deeply. We will not be in contact with what is happening in the present moment, and our relations with others will become shallow and impoverished.

Some days we may feel hollow, exhausted, and joyless, not really our true selves. On such days, even if we try to be in touch with others, our efforts will be in vain. The more we try, the more we fail. When this happens, we should stop trying to be in touch with what is outside of ourselves and come back to being in touch with ourselves, to "being alone." We should close the door onto society, come back to ourselves, and practice conscious breathing, observing deeply what is going on inside and around us. We accept all the phenomena we observe, say "hello" to them, smile at them. We do well to do simple things, like walking or sitting meditation, washing our clothes, cleaning the floor, making tea, and cleaning the bathroom in mindfulness. If we do these things, we will restore the richness of our spiritual life.

The Buddha was someone who lived an awakened life, dwelling constantly in the present moment in a relaxed and steady way. There was always a richness about him—a richness of freedom, joy, understanding, and love. Whether he was seated on a rocky crag of Vulture Peak, in the shade of the bamboo groves of Venuvana monastery, or under the thatched roof of his hut in Jetavana, Buddha was Buddha, unagitated, content, and of few words. Everyone could see that his presence contributed greatly to the harmony of the community. He was the main pillar of the community. For the monks and nuns, just to know that he was nearby had an active influence on the community. Many students of the Buddha, including hundreds of senior disciples, inspired similar confidence in those who observed them. King Prasenajit of Kosala once told the Buddha that what gave him so much confidence in the Buddha was the unhurried, calm, and joyful way of life of the monks and nuns who were practicing under his guidance.

If we live in mindfulness, we are no longer poor, because our practice of living in the present moment makes us rich in joy, peace, understanding, and love. Even when we encounter someone poor in spirit, we are able to look deeply and discover that person's depths and help him or her in an effective way.

When we watch an unwholesome movie or read a bad novel, if we are already poor in heart and mind and weak in mindfulness, that movie or book may irritate us and make us even poorer. But if we are rich in mindfulness, we will discover what lies in the depths of the film or the novel. We may be able to see deeply into the inner world of the person who directed the film or wrote the novel. Looking with the eyes of a literary or film critic, we can see things that most people do not see, and even a bad movie or book can teach us. Thus we are not impoverished by reading that novel or watching that film. Maintaining full awareness of each detail of the present moment, we are able to profit from it. This is the better way to live alone.

Internal Formations

The "Knowing the Better Way To Live Alone" gatha begins with the line: "Do not pursue the past." "Pursue the past" means to regret what has already come and gone. We regret the loss of the beautiful things of the past which we can no longer find in the present. Buddha commented on this line as follows: "When someone thinks how his body was in the past, how his feelings were in the past, how his perceptions were in the past, how his mental factors were in the past, how his consciousness was in the past, when he thinks like that and gives rise to a mind which is enslaved by those things which belong to the past, then that person is pursuing the past."

Buddha taught that we should not pursue the past "because the past no longer is." When we are lost in thoughts about the past, we lose the present. Life exists only in the present moment. To lose the present is to lose life. The Buddha's meaning is very clear: we must say good-bye to the past so that we may return to the present. To return to the present is to be in touch with life.

What dynamics in our consciousness compel us to go back and live with the images of the past? These forces are made up of internal formations (Sanskrit: *samyojana*), mental factors which arise in us and bind us. Things we see, hear, smell, taste, touch, imagine, or think can all give rise to internal formations—desire, irritation, anger, confusion, fear, anxiety, suspicion, and so on. Internal formations are present in the depths of the consciousness of each of us.

Internal formations influence our consciousness and our everyday behavior. They cause us to think, say, and do things that we may not even be aware of. Because they compel us in this way, they are also called fetters, because they bind us to acting in certain ways.

The commentaries usually mention nine kinds of internal formations: desire, hatred, pride, ignorance, stubborn views, attachment, doubt, jealousy, and selfishness. Among these, the fundamental internal formation is ignorance, the lack of clear-seeing. Ignorance is the raw material out of which the other internal formations are made. Although there are nine internal formations, because "desire" is always listed first, it is often used to represent all the internal formations. In the *Kaccana-Bhaddekaratta*, the monk Kaccana explains:

> My friends, what is meant by dwelling in the past? Someone thinks, "In the past my eyes were like that and the form (with

which my eyes were in contact) was like that," and thinking like this, he is bound by desire. Bound by desire there is a feeling of longing. This feeling of longing keeps him dwelling in the past.

Kaccana's commentary could make us think that the only internal formation holding one in the past is desire. But when Kaccana refers to "desire," he is using it to represent all the internal formations—hatred, doubt, jealousy, and so forth. All of these tie us and hold us back in the past.

Sometimes we only have to hear the name of someone who has wronged us in the past, and our internal formations from that time automatically take us back into the past, and we relive the suffering. The past is the home ground of both painful and happy memories. Being absorbed in the past is a way of being dead to the present moment. It is not easy to drop the past and return to living in the present. When we try to do it, we have to resist the force of the internal formations in us. We have to learn to transform our internal formations, so that we will be free to be attentive to the present moment.

The Present Is Also Made Up of the Past

The present contains the past. When we understand how our internal formations cause conflicts in us, we can see how the past is in the present moment, and we will no longer be overwhelmed by the past. When the Buddha said "Do not pursue the past," he was telling us not to be overwhelmed by the past. He did not mean that we should stop looking at the past in order to observe it deeply. When we review the past and observe it deeply, if we are standing firmly in the present, we are not overwhelmed by it. The materials of the past which make up the present become clear when they express themselves in the present. We can learn from them. If we observe these materials deeply, we can arrive at a new understanding of them. That is called "looking again at something old in order to learn something new."

If we know that the past also lies in the present, we understand that we are able to change the past by transforming the present. The ghosts of the past, which follow us into the present, also belong to the present moment. To observe them deeply, recognize their nature, and transform them, is to transform the past. The ghosts of the past are very real. They are the internal formations in us which are sometimes quietly asleep, while at other times they awaken suddenly and act in a strong way.

In Buddhism there is the Sanskrit term *anusaya*. "*Anu*" means "along with." *Saya* means "lying down." We could translate anusaya as "latent tendency." The internal formations continue to be with us, but they are lying asleep in the depths of our consciousness. We call them ghosts, but they are present in a very real way. According to the Vijñanavada school of Buddhism, *anusaya* are seeds which lie in everyone's *alaya* consciousness. An important part of the work of observation meditation is to be able to recognize the *anusaya* when they manifest, observe them deeply, and transform them.

Do Not Lose Yourself in the Future

Sometimes, because the present is so difficult, we give our attention to the future, hoping that the situation will improve in the future. Imagining the future will be better, we are better able to accept the suffering and hardship of the present. But at other times, thinking about the future may cause us a lot of fear and anxiety, and yet we cannot stop doing it. The reason we continue to think about the future, even when we do not want to, is due to the presence of internal formations. Although not yet here, the future is already producing ghosts which haunt us. In fact, these ghosts are not produced by the future or the past. It is our consciousness which creates them. The past and the future are creations of our consciousness.

The energies behind our thinking about the future are our hopes, dreams, and anxieties. Our hopes can be the result of our sufferings and failures. Because the present does not bring us happiness, we allow our minds to travel into the future. We hope that in the future, the situation will be brighter: "When someone thinks how his body will be in the future, how his feelings will be in the future, how his mental factors will be in the future, how his consciousness will be in the future..." Thinking in this way can give us the courage to accept failure and suffering in the present. The poet Tru Vu said that the future is the vitamin for the present. Hope brings us back some of the joys of life that we have lost.

We all know that hope is necessary for life. But according to Buddhism, hope can be an obstacle. If we invest our mind in the future, we will not have enough mental energy to face and transform the present. Naturally we have the right to make plans for the future, but making plans for the future does not mean to be swept away by daydreams. While we are making plans, our feet are firmly planted in the present. We can only build the future from the raw materials of the present.

The essential teaching of Buddhism is to be free of all desire for the future in order to come back with all our heart and mind into the present. To realize awakening means to arrive at a deep and full insight into reality, which is in the present moment. In order to return to the present and to be face to face with what is happening, we must look deeply into the heart of what is and experience its true nature. When we do so, we experience the deep understanding which can release us from suffering and darkness.

According to Buddhism, hell, paradise, *samsara*, and *nirvana* are all here in the present moment. To return to the present moment is to discover life and to realize the truth. All the Awakened Ones of the past have come to Awakening in the present moment. All the Awakened Ones of the present and the future will realize the fruit of Awakening in the present also. Only the present moment is real: "the past no longer is, and the future has not yet come."

If we do not stand firmly in the present moment, we may feel ungrounded when we look at the future.

We may think that in the future we will be alone, with no place of refuge and no one to help us. "When someone thinks how his body will be in the future, how his feelings will be in the future, how his mental factors will be in the future, how his consciousness will be in the future..." Such concerns about the future bring about unease, anxiety, and fear, and do not help us at all in taking care of the present moment. They just make our way of dealing with the present weak and confused. There is a Confucian saying that a person who does not know how to plan for the distant future will be troubled and perplexed by the near future. This is meant to remind us to care for the future, but not to be anxious and fearful about it. The best way of preparing for the future is to take good care of the present, because we know that if the present is made up of the past, then the future will be made up of the present. All we need to be responsible for is the present moment. Only the present is within our reach. To care for the present is to care for the future.

The Past and Future Both Lie in the Present

When we think about the past, feelings of regret or shame may arise. When we think about the future, feelings of desire or fear may come up. But all of these feelings arise in the present moment, and all of them affect the present moment. Most of the time, their effect does not contribute to our happiness or joy. We have to learn how to face these feelings. The main thing we need to remember is that the past and the future are both in the present, and, if we take hold of the present moment, then we also transform the past and the future.

How can we transform the past? In the past we may have said or done something destructive or harmful, and now we regret it. According to Buddhist psychology, regret is an "indeterminate emotion." This means that it can be either constructive or destructive. When we know that something we have said or done has caused harm, we may give rise to a mind of repentance, vowing that in the future we will not repeat the same mistake. In this case, our feeling of regret has a wholesome effect. If, on the other hand, the feeling of regret continues to disturb us, making it impossible for us to concentrate on anything else, taking all the peace and joy out of our lives, then that feeling of regret has an unwholesome effect.

When regret becomes unwholesome, we should first distinguish whether the cause was based on something we did or said, or on something we failed to do or say. If in the past, we said or did something destructive, we can call that an "error of commission." We did or said something with a lack of mindfulness, and it caused harm. Sometimes we commit an "error of omission." We did harm by not saying or doing what needed to be said or done, and that brought us regret and sorrow. Our lack of mindfulness was there, and its results are still present. Our pain, shame, and regret are an important part of that result. If we observe the present deeply and take hold of it, we can transform it. We do so by means of mindfulness, determination, and correct actions and speech. All these come about in the present moment. When we transform the present in this way, we also transform the past, and, at the same time, we build the future.

If we say that all is lost, everything is destroyed, or the suffering has already happened, we do not see that the past has become the present. Of course, the suffering has already been caused and the wound of that suffering can touch our very soul, but instead of lamenting about or suffering from what we have done in the past, we should take hold of the present and transform it. The traces of a bad drought can only be erased by a bountiful rainfall, and rain can only fall in the present moment.

Buddhist repentance is based on the understanding that wrongdoing originates in the mind. There is a gatha of repentance:

> All wrongdoings arise because of mind.
> If mind is transformed, can any wrongdoing remain?
> After repentance, my heart is light
> like the cloud floating free in the sky.

Because of our lack of mindfulness, because our mind was obscured by desire, anger, and jealousy, we acted wrongly. That is what is meant by, "All wrongdoings arise because of mind." But if the wrongdoing arose from our mind, it can also be transformed within our mind. If our mind is transformed, then the objects perceived by our mind will also be transformed. Such transformation is available if we know how to return to the present moment. Once we have transformed our mind, our heart will be as light as a floating cloud, and we become a source of peace and joy for ourselves and others. Yesterday, perhaps out of foolishness or anger, we said something which made our mother sad. But today our mind is transformed and our heart light, and we can see our mother smiling at us, even if she is no longer alive. If we can smile within ourselves, our mother can also smile with us.

If we can transform the past, we can also transform the future. Our anxieties and fears for the future make the present dark. There is no doubt that the future will be black too, because we know that the future is made up of the present. Taking care of the present is the best way to take care of the future. Sometimes, because we are so concerned about what will happen the next day, we toss and turn all night, unable to sleep. We worry that if we cannot sleep during the night, we will be tired the next day and unable to perform to the best of our ability. The more we worry, the more difficult it is for us to sleep. Our worries and fears for the future destroy the present. But if we stop thinking about tomorrow and just stay in bed and follow our breathing, really enjoying the opportunity we have to rest, not only will we savor the moments of peace and joy under the warm blankets, but we will fall asleep quite easily and naturally. That kind of sleep is a big help for making the next day a success.

When we hear that the forests of our planet are diseased and dying so rapidly, we may feel anxious. We are concerned for the future, because we are aware of what is happening in the present moment. Our awareness can motivate us to do something to halt the destruction of our environment. Obviously, our concern for the future is different from worry and anxiety which only drain us. We have to know how to enjoy the presence of beautiful, healthy trees in order to be able to do something to protect and preserve them.

When we throw a banana peel into the garbage, if we are mindful, we know that the peel will become compost and be reborn as a tomato or a lettuce salad in just a few months. But when we throw a plastic bag into the garbage, thanks to our awareness, we know that a plastic bag will not become a tomato or a salad very quickly. Some kinds of garbage need four or five hundred years to decompose. Nuclear waste needs a quarter of a million years before it stops being harmful and returns to the soil. Living in the present moment in an awakened way, looking after the present moment with all our heart, we will not do things which destroy the future. That is the most concrete way to do what is constructive for the future.

In our everyday life, we may also produce poisons for our minds, and these poisons destroy not only us but also those who live with us, in the present and in the future too. Buddhism talks about three poisons: desire, hatred, and ignorance. In addition, there are other poisons whose capacity to do harm is very great: jealousy, prejudice, pride, suspicion, and obstinacy.

In our day-to-day relationships with ourselves, others, and our environment, any or all of these poisons can manifest, blaze up, and destroy our peace and joy, as well as the peace and joy of those around us. These poisons can linger and pollute our minds, causing bitter consequences in the future.

So to live in the present moment is also to accept and face these poisons as they arise, manifest, and return to the unconscious, and to practice observation meditation in order to transform them. This is a Buddhist practice. To live in the present is also to see the wonderful and wholesome things in order to nourish and protect them. Happiness is the direct result of facing things and being in touch. That happiness is the material from which a beautiful future is manufactured.

Life Is Found in the Present

To return to the present is to be in contact with life. Life can be found only in the present moment, because "the past no longer is" and "the future has not yet come." Buddhahood, liberation, awakening, peace, joy, and happiness can only be found in the present moment. Our appointment with life is in the present moment. The place of our appointment is right here, in this very place.

According to the *Avatamsaka Sutra*, time and space are not separate. Time is made up of space, and space is made up of time. When we speak about spring, we usually think of time, but spring is also space. When it is spring in Europe, it is winter in Australia.

Holding up their cup of tea, those who attend the tea meditation breathe and recite the following gatha:

This cup of tea in my two hands—
mindfulness is held uprightly.
My mind and body dwell
in the very here and now.

When we drink tea in mindfulness, we practice coming back to the present moment to live our life right here. When our mind and our body are fully in the present moment, then the steaming cup of tea appears clearly to us. We know it is a wonderful aspect of existence. At that time we are really in contact with the cup of tea. It is only at times like this that life is really present.

Peace, joy, liberation, awakening, happiness, Buddhahood, the source—everything we long for and seek after can only be found in the present moment. To abandon the present moment in order to look for these things in the future is to throw away the substance and hold onto the shadow. In Buddhism, "aimlessness" (*apranihita)* is taught as a way to help the practitioner stop pursuing the future and return wholly to the present. Aimlessness is sometimes called wishlessness, and it is one of the "three doors to liberation." (The other two are emptiness and signlessness.) To be able to stop pursuing the future allows us to realize that all the wonderful things we seek are present in us, in the present moment. Life is not a particular place or a destination. Life is a path. To practice walking meditation is to go without needing to arrive. Every step can bring us peace, joy, and liberation. That is why we walk in the spirit of aimlessness. There is no way to liberation, peace, and joy; peace and joy are themselves the way. Our appointment with the

Buddha, with liberation, and with happiness is here and now. We should not miss this appointment.

Buddhism teaches a way of breathing which gives us the capacity of making body and mind one in order to be face to face with life. This is called "oneness of body and mind." That is why every meditator begins by practicing the Sutra on the Full Awareness of Breathing (Anapanasati Sutta).

But to come back to the present does not mean to be carried away by what is happening in the present. The sutra teaches us to observe life deeply and be in touch with the present moment, and see all the sufferings and the wonders of the present. Yet we must do so in mindfulness, maintaining a high degree of awareness in order not to be carried away by, or caught in, desire for or aversion to what is happening in the present.

> Looking deeply at life as it is
> in the very here and now,
> the practitioner dwells
> in stability and freedom.

"Stability and freedom" refer to the contentment and tranquillity of not being carried away by anything whatsoever. Stability and ease are two characteristics of nirvana. The Pali version of this verse uses two terms, asamkuppam and asamhiram. Asamkuppam means "unwavering, unshakable, immovable, unexcitable." Sanghadeva translates it as "firm and unwavering." Dharmapala translates it as "stable." Asamhiram means, literally, "not folded together, not restrained, not collected, not carried away by anything." Sanghadeva, the monk and translator of the *Madhyamagama*, translated *asamhiram* into Chinese as "non-existing *(wu yu)*," which is not exact. The monk Dharmapala, in *The Elder Sutra*, translated *asamhiram* as "not fettered." "Fettered" here means "imprisoned." So "not fettered" means "not caught" or "in freedom."

Being in contact with life in the present moment, we observe deeply what is. Then we are able to see the impermanent and selfless nature of all that is. Impermanence and selflessness are not negative aspects of life but the very foundations on which life is built. Impermanence is the constant transformation of things. Without impermanence, there can be no life. Selflessness is the interdependent nature of all things. Without interdependence, nothing could exist. Without the sun, the clouds, and the Earth, the tulip could not be. We often feel sad about the impermanence and selflessness of life, because we forget that, without impermanence and selflessness, life cannot be. To be aware of impermanence and selflessness does not take away the joy of being alive. On the contrary, it adds healthiness, stability, and freedom. It is because people cannot see the impermanent and selfless nature of things that they suffer. They take what is impermanent as permanent and that what is selfless as having a self.

Looking deeply into a rose, we can see its impermanent nature quite clearly. At the same time, we can still see its beauty and value its preciousness. Because we perceive its fragile and impermanent nature, we may see that flower as even more beautiful and precious. The more fragile something is, the more beautiful and precious it is—for example, a rainbow, a sunset, a cereus cactus flowering by night, a falling star. Looking at the sun rising over Vulture Peak, at the town of Vesali, at a field of ripe, golden rice, the Buddha saw their beauty and told Ananda so.

Seeing deeply the impermanent nature of those beautiful things, their transformation and disappearance, the Buddha did not suffer or despair. We, too, by observing deeply and seeing impermanence and selflessness in all that is, can overcome despair and suffering and experience the preciousness of the miracles of everyday life—a glass of clear water, a cool breeze, a step taken in ease and freedom. All these are wonderful things, although they are impermanent and selfless.

Life is suffering, but it is also wonderful. Sickness, old age, death, accident, starvation, unemployment, and natural disasters cannot be avoided in life. But, if our understanding is deep and our mind free, we can accept these things with tranquillity, and the suffering will already be greatly lessened. This is not to say we should close our eyes before suffering. By being in contact with suffering, we give rise to and nourish our natural love and compassion. Suffering becomes the element which nourishes our love and compassion, and so we are not afraid of it. When our heart is filled with love and compassion, we will act in ways to help relieve the sufferings of others.

If the human species has been able to make any progress, it is because of our heart of love and compassion. We need to learn from compassionate beings how to develop the practice of deep observation for the sake of others. Then others will be able to learn from us the way to live in the present and see the impermanent and selfless nature of all that is. This insight will lighten suffering.

Fear of the unexpected leads many people to live a constricted and anxious life. No one can know in advance the misfortunes which may happen to us and our loved ones, but if we learn to live in an awakened way, living deeply every moment of our life, treating those who are close to us with gentleness and understanding, then we will have nothing to regret when something happens to us or to them. Living in the present moment, we are able to be in touch with life's wonderful, refreshing, and health-giving phenomena, which allow us to heal the wounds in ourselves. Every day we become more wonderful, fresh, and healthy.

A Life of Peace, Freedom, and Joy

To practice a life of deep observation according to the teachings of the Buddha is to have a life of peace, freedom, and joy, and to realize complete liberation. The "Knowing the Better Way to Live Alone" gatha reminds us that we cannot avoid death and advises us to be diligent in the practice today, for tomorrow it will be too late. Death comes unexpectedly, and there is no way to bargain with it. If we live observing everything deeply in the present moment, we learn to live in peace and joy with freedom and stability. If we continue to practice diligently in this way, peace, joy, and stability will grow every day until we realize complete liberation.

When there is complete liberation, death can no longer harm us. A life like this will bring joy to our dear ones and others. The material of stability and release is also the element of liberation. Liberation is the fruit of deep observation which leads to the realization of the impermanent and selfless nature of all that is. By observing at a deep level, we can defeat death, because the observation of impermanence can lead us to transcend the boundaries of birth and death. When we look at all that is in the universe and all those dear to us, we see that there is nothing eternal and unchanging that we can call "I" or "self."

Transcending Birth and Death

We often think that birth is that which does not exist coming into existence, and that death is that which does exist ceasing to exist. When we look deeply at things, we see that this idea about birth and death is mistaken in many respects. No phenomenon whatsoever can come into existence out of nothing, and no phenomenon which exists can become nothing. Things are ceaselessly transforming. The cloud does not die; it only becomes rain. The rain is not born; it is only the transformation and continuation of the cloud. Leaves, a pair of shoes, joy, and sorrow all conform to this principle of no-birth and no-death. To think that after death we no longer exist is a narrow view which in Buddhism is called the "nihilistic view." The narrow view that after death we continue to exist without changing is called the "view of permanence." Reality transcends both permanence and annihilation.

The Buddha taught us to look directly into the elements which combine together to constitute our body, in order to see the nature of these elements and transcend the idea of "self"—whether it is the idea of a permanent, indestructible self, or the idea of a self subject to complete annihilation after we die. The sutra says: "Someone who studies and learns about the Awakened One, the teachings of love and understanding, and the community which lives in harmony and awareness, who knows about noble teachers and their teachings and practices these teachings, does not think, 'This body is myself. I am this body. These feelings are myself. I am these feelings. This perception is myself. I am this perception. This mental factor is myself. I am this mental factor. This consciousness is myself. I am this consciousness,' then that person [does not go back to the past, does not think ahead to the future and] is not being swept away by the present."

The five elements which combine together to become the thing we call self are form (the body), feelings, perceptions, mental factors, and consciousness. If we look penetratingly into the substance of these elements and see their impermanent and interdependent nature, we naturally see that there is no entity we can call "self." All five elements are constantly transforming. They are never born and never die. There is no element that goes from nothingness into existence nor any element which goes from existence into nothingness. The thing which we think of as "I" is not born and does not die. We do not identify "I" with the body whether that body is developing or degenerating, nor with the feelings which change at every moment. Similarly we do not identify with our perceptions and our consciousness. We are not bound or limited by these five elements. We see that if these elements really are not born or destroyed, then we need no longer be oppressed by death. This insight enables us to transcend birth and death.

When the sutra refers to someone who "practices according to the teachings of the Noble Ones," it means someone who lives in the present and observes deeply in order to see life's impermanent and selfless nature. The Buddha taught that "we must practice diligently today for tomorrow will be too late; death comes unexpectedly and there is no bargaining with it." Observing deeply, we can realize the birthless and deathless nature of things, and there is nothing more which can frighten us, not even death. We directly overcome birth and death, when, by deep observation and realization of impermanence and selflessness, we pierce through false ideas about the nature of existence. Once we overcome death, we no longer need to "bargain with death." We can smile, take the hand of death, and go for a walk together.

The life called the "brahma-faring life" of a monk or a nun can lead to the realization of the birthless and deathless nature of all that is. That realization is the substance of liberation. That is why in the *Kaccana-Bhaddekaratta Sutra*, it is emphasized that the practice of living alone is the basis of the brahma-faring life of a monk or a nun. It is also the basis of life for all of us.

Appendix

The following is the translation of the
Bhaddekaratta Gatha seen in the *God of the Forest
Hot Springs Sutra (Madhyamagama* 165), the
Shakyan Hermitage Sutra (M 166), and the *Sutra
Spoken by Ananda (M* 167).

> Do not think of the past.
> Do not worry about the future.
> Things of the past have died.
> The future has not arrived.
> What is happening in the present
> should be observed deeply.
> The Wise Ones live according to this
> and dwell in stability and freedom.
> If one practices the teachings
> of the Wise Ones,
> why should one be afraid of death?
> If we do not understand this,
> there is no way to avoid
> the great pain of the final danger.
> To practice diligently day and night,
> one should regularly recite
> the *Bhaddekaratta Gatha.*

The following *Bhaddekaratta Gatha* is seen in the
translation of the *Great Reverence Sutra,* which is
no. 77 in the *Taisho Revised Tripitaka:*

> Not thinking about the past,
> not seeking something in the future—
> the past has already died,
> the future is not in our hands—

we should observe deeply
and contemplate
what is in the present moment.
The person who constantly practices
the way of the wise ones
has awakened understanding.
Diligently practicing,
without wavering and
released from care,
what does he fear at the time of death?
If he does not practice diligently,
how can he overcome death and its armies?
Truly we should practice
according to this wonderful gatha.

About the Author

Thich Nhat Hanh is a Vietnamese Buddhist monk, ordained in the Zen tradition. He is author of *Zen Keys*, *The Sun My Heart*, *Being Peace*, and many other works.

About the Translator

Annabel Laity is a school teacher and Buddhist practitioner, presently living in Plum Village in France.

About Parallax Press

Parallax Press publishes books and tapes on Buddhism and related subjects for contemporary readers. We carry all books by Thich Nhat Hanh in English. For a copy of our free catalogue, please write to:

Parallax Press

P. O. Box 7355

Berkeley, California 94707